The Wonder of Christmas
Once You Believe, Anything Is Possible

The Wonder of Christmas
Once You Believe, Anything Is Possible

The Wonder of Christmas
978-1-5018-2322-0 *Book*
978-1-5018-2323-7 *eBook*
978-1-5018-2324-4 *Large Print*

The Wonder of Christmas: Leader Guide
978-1-5018-2325-1 *Book*
978-1-5018-2326-8 *eBook*

The Wonder of Christmas: DVD
978-1-5018-2329-9

The Wonder of Christmas: Devotions for the Season
978-1-5018-2327-5 *Book*
978-1-5018-2328-2 *eBook*

The Wonder of Christmas: Children's Leader Guide
978-1-5018-2336-7

The Wonder of Christmas: Youth Study Book with Leader Helps
978-1-5018-2334-3 *Book*
978-1-5018-2335-0 *eBook*

The Wonder of Christmas: Worship Planning
978-1-5018-2337-4 *Flash Drive*
978-1-5018-2338-1 *Download*

Ed Robb & Rob Renfroe

THE
Wonder
OF CHRISTMAS

ONCE YOU BELIEVE,
ANYTHING IS POSSIBLE

Abingdon Press / Nashville

THE WONDER OF CHRISTMAS
Once You Believe, Anything Is Possible

This book is printed on elemental chlorine-free paper.

Library of Congress Cataloging-in-Publication data applied for.

978-1-5018-2322-0

Scripture quotations marked NRSV are taken from the New Revised Standard Version of the Bible, copyright 1989, Division of Christian Education of the National Council of the Churches of Christ in the United States of America. Used by permission. All rights reserved.

Scripture quotations marked KJV are taken from The Authorized (King James) Version. Rights in the Authorized Version in the United Kingdom are vested in the Crown. Reproduced by permission of the Crown's patentee, Cambridge University Press.

Scripture quotations marked NKJV are taken from the New King James Version®. Copyright © 1982 by Thomas Nelson, Inc. Used by permission. All rights reserved.

Scripture quotations marked NIV are taken from the Holy Bible, Today's New International Version®. Copyright © 2001, 2005 Biblica, Inc.™. All rights reserved worldwide. Used by permission of Biblica, Inc.

Scripture quotations marked NASB are taken from the New American Standard Bible®, Copyright © 1960, 1962, 1963, 1968, 1971, 1972, 1973, 1975, 1977, 1995 by The Lockman Foundation. Used by permission. (www.Lockman.org)

Scripture quotations marked NLT are taken from the Holy Bible, New Living Translation, copyright © 1996, 2004, 2007. Used by permission of Tyndale House Publishers, Inc., Carol Stream, Illinois 60188. All rights reserved.

16 17 18 19 20 21 22 23 24 25 — 10 9 8 7 6 5 4 3 2 1
MANUFACTURED IN THE UNITED STATES OF AMERICA

Contents

Introduction

There are many things we can conclude about God from creation. Look at the immensity of the universe, and we can deduce that the God who created it must be incredibly powerful. Look at its order and its beauty, and we can surmise that the mind that holds it together must be remarkable beyond all imagining. Listen to the conscience within you, and you can infer that the One who brought you into existence must be moral. But one thing we could never know about God from the created world is how much he loves us. This is what Christmas proves for us—that God cares about each of us personally and passionately.

The psalmist asked, "What are human beings that you are mindful of them?" (Psalm 8:4 NRSV). If there is a God great enough to bring the universe into existence, why would we be given a second thought? That's what the psalmist wanted to know. And the thought is even more incredulous to us. We know about the immensity of creation in ways the psalmist did not. We live on a small planet, revolving around an unimpressive sun, in a galaxy that contains three hundred billion stars. And there are between two hundred and three hundred billion galaxies.

Indeed, who are we that God would be mindful of us? Who would dream that the God of the universe would think about us—much less want to have a relationship with us? Who would have imagined that God would come among us not as a ruler to be feared but as a servant to care for our needs?

Who would have guessed that Jesus would weep at a dead friend's grave as he did with Lazarus or stop for a blind man along the road as he did with Bartimaeus or touch and heal a leper who said to him, "I know you can make me well if only you are willing" (Matthew 8:2, author's paraphrase)?

Who would have dreamed that God would be willing to take on human flesh? That God would experience our pain and our grief? That God would bear our shame and die for our sins?

And why? Because God loves us. Because God loves *you*.

There are many things we might conclude about God apart from Christmas. But without Christmas we could never fully know the wonder of God's love.

Christmas shows us that every person matters to God. You matter to God—more than you can imagine, more than you will allow yourself to believe. You matter to God!

A popular song tells us "it's the most wonderful time of the year." And that's true; Christmas is wonderful. But it's not because of caroling or parties. It's because of the wonder of what Christmas tells us: God loves us and has come among us. This is the wonder of Christmas!

Each week during Advent we will explore one of four elements of the Christmas story that teach us about the wonder of God's great love for us:

- a star
- a name
- a manger
- a promise

As we look to the Christmas story and the stories of real people today, we will rediscover that the true wonder of Christmas is found in the love of Christ and made real in our hearts when we share that love with others.

Each chapter contains questions for reflection, scriptures for meditation, and a prayer intended to assist you in reflecting on what God is doing in your heart during this season. A special reading that may be used when lighting a home Advent wreath is also provided (see pages 11-12 for more about using an Advent wreath to prepare for Jesus' birth). Whether you read these chapters on your own or as part of a group study, may this exploration of the Wonder of Christmas enrich and prepare you spiritually for the coming of the most wonderful gift ever given: God's Son, Jesus Christ.

Although much about our world seems filled with darkness, danger, and uncertainty, we have the certain hope that a light shines in the darkness—and darkness has not overcome it. This season may you embrace and celebrate the true wonder of Christmas, believing that because of God's great love and light in Jesus Christ, anything is possible!

Using an Advent Wreath to Celebrate the Wonder of Christmas

Advent wreaths, which were originally used in the home and became popular in churches in the midtwentieth century, are a wonderful way not only to mark the four weeks in Advent as you prepare for Christ's coming but also to help you recognize and celebrate the wonder of Christmas.

If you do not have an Advent wreath, you can make one by placing four purple pillar candles in a circular Styrofoam base, attaching greenery around the wreath. Or you may simply put the candles in candleholders placed in a circle.

The circular wreath symbolizes the eternity of God, and the purple candles symbolize the royalty of the coming King, Jesus. (If you like, one of the candles can be pink to symbolize joy.) Complete your wreath by placing a white candle in the center to represent Christ, the light of the world.

Each Sunday in Advent, light one new candle (plus any previously lit), and use the reading provided for that week (found at the end of each chapter). Whether doing this on your own or with family members, you will find that the readings help to focus your thoughts on four wonder-filled elements of the Christmas story:[*]

- *The Star*: Hope in knowing that Jesus is the answer for our deepest need
- *The Name*: Peace in knowing that Jesus is "the God who saves"
- *The Manger*: Love that sent Jesus to be born in a humble manger
- *The Promise*: Joy that is ours in the promised Christ, God with us

---

[*] The order and exact wording of the four themes vary among churches, but we have chosen this order for *The Wonder of Christmas*. Regardless of the order used, the Advent wreath reminds us of the symbolism and meaning of Christmas.

1.

The Wonder of a Star

1.

The Wonder of a Star

ROB RENFROE

"Where is the one who has been born king of the Jews? We saw his star when it rose and have come to worship him."

Matthew 2:2 NIV

My wife, Peggy, has a habit that drives me crazy—and brings me lots of joy. Wherever we are, whatever we're doing, however late we might be, she'll stop and take a picture—

several pictures. Usually her unplanned photography is preceded by her stopping, bending over, and saying, "Isn't that amazing?" Often what has grabbed her attention is something I have already passed by without noticing. Even when she points it out, it seems rather mundane and ordinary to me. It's just a rock on a path or a shell on the beach or some berries in a bush or some fungus on a decaying tree branch.

Here's the strange thing. When we get home and she enlarges the picture and shows it to me, I see it—the interplay of different colors in a stone she spotted lying in a riverbed; the pattern of stripes on the wings of a bug she saw crawling on a blade of grass; the design of a flower's petals as intricate and delicate as the stitching of a quilt; the brilliant hues of berries in a field, hiding their glory under a carpet of wild grass. When she shows these things to me, I can see the beauty that she saw, the magnificence of little things I had walked by and missed.

Peggy is an artist—she paints, creates, and imagines. Like every artist, she sees the world with a sense of curiosity and appreciation—actually, it is the gift of wonder. The gift of wonder is the ability to be amazed by little things—to see more when other people see less; to be surprised again by the beauty you've seen a hundred times, feeling about it the way you did the first time you saw it—and to wonder how life could give you such a marvelous gift.

As we explore the wonder of Christmas together in the coming weeks, you are invited to see the world—and what God has done—through the gift of wonder; to believe there is more to this world than the eye beholds; to look for the beauty in what God has done and allow yourself to be amazed by a story you've heard a hundred times; to come to this season with a spirit of curiosity, trusting that if you will slow down and open your heart, Creation's Artist will astonish you with gifts that are waiting for you.

A passage from a sermon written by Frederick Buechner, "The Face in the Sky," is a good way to begin talking about the wonder of Christmas:

> Those who believe in God can never in a way be sure of him again. Once they have seen him in a stable, they can never be sure where he will appear or to what lengths he will go or to what ludicrous depths of self-humiliation he will descend in his wild pursuit of man. If holiness and the awful power and majesty of God were present in this least auspicious of all events, this birth of a peasant's child, then there is no place or time so lowly and earthbound but that holiness can be present there too.[1]

Buechner is saying that once you believe in Christmas, the world becomes a place of wonder—a place where God is waiting for us. Waiting to show us the beauty and the goodness of life. Waiting to show us something that will stop us in our tracks, speak to our hearts, and amaze us. Waiting to show us something that will lead us to God. But we must have eyes to see.

Let's begin by exploring the wonder of a star that first heralded the coming of Christ into the world—a star that captivated the attention of certain wise men who appeared after the birth of Jesus to worship him. What can we learn from them that can help to awaken us to the wonder of Christmas?

The Eyes to See

Though the wise men play an important part in the nativity story, the truth is that we do not know much about them. In all likelihood, they arrived a good deal later than the shepherds. We are told in Matthew 2:11 that the wise men found the family in a "house," so there had been sufficient time for the family to move from the stable into a more permanent dwelling.

Matthew's Gospel tells us they were from the east (Matthew 2:1)—which would have been in the direction of Babylon and ancient Persia. The Greek word *magos*, which is used to describe them in the original text, indicates they were scholar-priests.[2] Certainly they would have been highly educated and culturally sophisticated. Without a doubt they enjoyed positions of privilege. The fact that they were able to make the kind of trip that is implied in Matthew's account tells us that they were men of great wealth.

Once you believe in Christmas,
the world becomes a
place of wonder. But we must
have eyes to see.

These wise men had all of the material wealth that anyone could have desired, yet still there was something inside them that wanted more—something that compelled them to travel hundreds of miles through foreign lands and barren terrain on the back of a camel; something that told them their lives were incomplete, and they were made for more.

Most of us sense we were made for more. We feel that something is missing—that we need something more for our lives to be right. But not all of us recognize what this need truly is. In fact, many people who yearn for something more focus on getting more of the same, thinking that more of what they already have will satisfy the need. So they set out on a journey to acquire more wealth, more success, more recognition, more stuff, more pleasure—more of everything that has already left them unsatisfied and unfulfilled. As a result, their life's journey becomes nothing but a distraction, keeping them from finding the "more" they are longing for.

The wise men were wise because they knew that what they needed was not more of the same but more in the sense of something different—something they had not yet experienced. The longing within was a yearning for something more than this world could provide. So they set out on a spiritual quest to find something that could fill the longing within their souls.

We like to think that we have come so far as a human race, and in many ways we have. But the most important truth about us human beings has not changed: wealth, power, positions of privilege, and physical pleasures are not enough to satisfy the deepest longings of our hearts. Something within the wise men knew that they were made for more, and something inside you knows the same. Something within you wants more than this world can provide. That's why you can have everything and still feel empty inside.

Ecclesiastes 3:11 tells us that God has placed eternity in our hearts. Even if your head has forgotten this, your heart still remembers. At your core, you are a spiritual being. Because you are more than the stuff of this earth, the stuff of this earth will never be enough to satisfy your heart or give you peace. You long for a profound connection to realities that are eternal and spiritual. As the psalmist wrote, "Deep calls to deep" (Psalm 42:7 NIV). At some time in our lives we all feel it—something deep within telling us not to be satisfied with the shallow things of life because we were made for more.

Many of us lose that yearning along life's way. We become distracted with making a living and raising kids and paying the bills and a million other things. But then Christmas comes along, and as we're gathered around the tree we feel it again—the hope that comes from believing that maybe God can be found in a manger and in the mundane places of our lives. We feel both the dissatisfaction with what is and the courage to believe that maybe our lives can be different— better than they have been. Christmas brings the wonder of seeing the world anew, as an artist perceiving that there is more to reality than meets the eye, more than the things that can be seen and touched. And once again we feel deep calling to deep, telling us we were made for something more.

The wise men were wise because they were not blinded by the fact that they had everything. They did not allow their souls to be anesthetized by possessions and success. They wanted more. But they were wise for another reason: they recognized the sign that God placed before them.

When they arrived in Jerusalem, the wise men asked King Herod: "Where is the one who has been born king of the Jews? We saw his star when it rose and have come to worship him" (Matthew 2:2 NIV). What is remarkable about the wise men is not that they saw the star. Everyone who looked into the night sky saw the same star. No, what made them wise is that they recognized the star for what it was: a sign that could lead them to God.

Scholars still debate what the star actually was. Some have suggested it was a nova, a newborn star that burned exceedingly bright for a short period of time. Others have said it was a comet. In recent times some have posited that it might have been the conjunction of Saturn and Jupiter, appearing to the naked eye as a single, brilliant star.

Once scientists agree upon a definitive answer, they still will know less about that star than the wise men if they do not recognize that it was more than a cosmic phenomenon. Whatever else it was, it was a sign that could lead men and women to Christ.

Christmas brings the wonder
of seeing the world anew, as an
artist perceiving that there is
more to reality than meets the
eye, more than the things that
can be seen and touched.

Life is full of signs. *Your* life is full of signs. Take, for example, the struggle you experience inside. You so want to be unselfish and accepting and forgiving, but when you're honest, you find it hard to be the person you want to be and easy to be the kind of person you despise. What kind of sign do you think that is? It's a sign that, like the rest of us, you're made in the image of God yet flawed inside and in need of help. It is a sign pointing you to God.

Here's another sign you've experienced if you are a parent: the way you felt when you first held your newborn child. How impossible it seemed that anything so wonderful could come from you. Sure, you understood the biology and the genetics, but when you looked into that tiny face and felt your child's heartbeat next to yours, every argument about life being meaningless and accidental seemed ridiculous. What kind of sign is that? It is a sign that life has meaning and is grounded in something larger than itself. It is a sign pointing you to God.

Maybe for you the sign is how you feel when you gaze upon the beauty of a sunset or stand surrounded by the majesty of the mountains. Maybe it's the stirrings you experience as you listen to great music and find yourself longing for something—you're not even sure what. You can't explain it, but there is a sense of wonder telling you that there is another dimension to who you are—something that science and reason alone cannot explain.

Maybe a sign has come in a time of tragedy and suffering, when you seemed lost and alone but found yourself buoyed by a strength you knew was not your own. Some little act of kindness, perhaps from someone you barely knew, told you that someone cared and that life could be good again. And it was enough to get you through the darkness and pain.

On Christmas morning as you open presents with family and friends and find yourself experiencing more pleasure from the gifts you've given than from the gifts you've received, what do you think that is? It is a sign that at the heart of reality there is a heart of compassion that loves to give and share life with others. It is a sign pointing you to God.

Life is full of signs, and what distinguishes the wise from the foolish is the ability to recognize them for what they are. I pray that, like the wise men, you will have the gift of wonder this Christmas—the eyes of an artist that see the beautiful patterns and remarkable colors God has placed in your life. And I pray that you will be amazed at all God has done and is doing to reach out and reveal himself to you.

The Courage to Follow

The wise men not only had the eyes to see the star as a sign, they also had the courage to follow the sign until they found Jesus.

What I find most amazing about this story is not that the wise men traveled to Bethlehem; it is that no one—other than their own entourage, which would have been traveling with them—went with them. When they first went to King Herod in Jerusalem and told him about the star, he did not scoff, saying "You've got it wrong. There is no prophecy," or, "You're mistaken. The star means nothing. It's not a sign." No, he believed their report.

In Matthew's Gospel we read, "When King Herod heard this he was disturbed, and all Jerusalem with him" (2:3 NIV). Herod called the chief priests and asked them where the Messiah was to be born. They told him it would be in Bethlehem of Judea.

Why do you think Herod was so disturbed? Because he could see the star for himself—as could the chief priests and all of Jerusalem. They recognized the sign for what it was. But when the wise men went to find the newborn king, the Messiah, the Scriptures do not indicate that anyone from Jerusalem went with them. This astounds me. Why didn't any of the people go to Bethlehem to check out this baby—even if there was only the slightest chance that he might be the Messiah? After all, they were familiar with Isaiah's prophecy:

> *For to us a child is born,*
> *to us a child is given,...*
> *And he will be called*
> *Wonderful Counselor, Mighty God,*
> *Everlasting Father, Prince of Peace*
> *Isaiah 9:6 NIV*

It is almost inconceivable to think that no one went with the wise men to see Jesus, but that is what we can assume from Matthew's account. The question is why?

Perhaps they were too busy. It sounds crazy to say they were too busy to find the Messiah, but isn't that the excuse we often make? "I've got too much going on in my life to spend time on spiritual matters. I've got responsibilities; I can't just rearrange my schedule to make time to pray and read the Bible, much less join a Bible study or small group." Often we allow busyness with matters that are temporal to keep us from seeking the eternal. We respond to pressing matters that appear "urgent" and fail to pursue what is truly and forever important. So it's not impossible that a king and his chief priests thought themselves so occupied with their busy schedules and pressing responsibilities that they did not make time to go with those who were wise enough to seek the one born King of the Jews. But here's what I think the real reason was: they were afraid. No doubt they knew that if the Messiah truly had come into the world, then they would have to change their beliefs, their priorities, and their lives. That would explain why, when the wise men set out for Bethlehem, Herod and the others stayed in Jerusalem, doing what they had always done, living how they had always lived, and being who they had always been.

We do the same thing. When we're angry and want to stay that way, we stay away from Jesus because we know he will make us change. When we're selfish and proud and want to stay that way, we stay away from Jesus because we know he'll make us change. When we're full of self-pity and want to hold on to our hurt, we stay away from Jesus because we know he'll make us change. When we're unfaithful to what we know is right because that is easier than having integrity, we stay away from Jesus because we know he will make us change. Why? Because he loves us!

When we want to be in charge of our destiny and refuse to get off the throne of our lives, we stay away from Jesus because we are disturbed by the idea that he will tell us to step down and let him change our lives. And here's the crazy part. Every time I've gone to Jesus and he has made me change, I have loved what it felt like to be forgiven. I have loved being free of bitterness, letting go of selfishness, and getting rid of fear and pride. Every time I have let go of what's holding on to me so that I could take hold of Jesus, it has brought me peace and joy.

But let's be honest. King Herod knew there was room for only one on the throne, and we know the same thing. It's either Jesus or us. So, sometimes when we recognize the signs for what they are, we still choose not to follow them to Jesus because of our fear.

Make no mistake about it: Jesus was not born into our world to be oohed and ahhed over as a newborn baby or a young toddler. He was born King of the Jews—and of all humankind. He came to rule. When you know that, it requires courage to come to him. When you sense that he may take from you what you have trusted for your sense of worth and security and require you to trust him alone for a sense of well-being, a very natural and understandable reaction is fear. King Herod must have wondered, "If there is a new king in my place, who will I be without my position and my crown? If he is indeed the king, will I be expected to be his servant?"

We must all ask ourselves a similar question: If Jesus takes the throne of my life, what will I be called to give up? This leads to other questions. Who will I be if I am no longer the ruler of my own life, defined by my successes and accomplishments and free to do whatever I desire? If Jesus requires that I let go of habits and patterns that have brought me comfort and peace of mind, will his grace be sufficient? What if he calls me to forsake my plans and pursue a different purpose? Will I be willing to make such a change and trust him? Will Jesus reigning in me be enough if that is all I have?

These are not only valid questions, they are questions we must ask before we truly trust in Christ. They are questions that require enough courage for us to say, "If he takes all I have and gives me only himself, it will be enough and more." Not all of us possess the courage to go to Jesus without knowing what he will take from us when he takes his place on the throne of our lives. So many stay behind as Herod and the priests did, letting others go to find the King.

The Humility to Worship

The wise men had the eyes to see and the courage to follow. But most important of all, they had the humility to worship.

"On coming to the house, they saw the child with his mother Mary, and they bowed down and worshiped him" (Matthew 2:11a NIV). That must have been an interesting sight. We think of the wise men as kings, though the Bible doesn't say that they were. As we've established, certainly they were men of education, wealth, and power. And we can be sure that friends and servants were traveling with them, along with a huge train of supplies. Each wise man would have brought his own caravan. Yet upon entering a humble house in an occupied country, these men of influence and power fell to their knees, bowed their heads, and worshiped the child of a poor Jewish family.

Why did they worship? This newborn child had done nothing yet. He had no army, no subjects, no kingdom. He had not yet performed a miracle or spoken the words of a prophet. In fact, he had done nothing other than what any other newborn child would have done. And still they worshiped him. Why? The answer is that we do not worship God primarily for what God has done but for who God is. I imagine that as they stepped into a humble home and looked at a poor couple's child, they recognized that Jesus was and is God—and that they were God's creations. He was and is life; they were mortal. He was and is love, righteousness, and beauty; it is because of him that we know what true love and beauty are.

God put a star in the sky, and the wise men saw it for what it was:

> star of wonder, star of light,
> star with royal beauty bright,
> westward leading, still proceeding,
> guide us to thy perfect light[3]

Once they stood in the presence of that light, they fell to their knees, humbled their hearts, and worshiped Jesus.

John's Gospel does not include a traditional nativity story as Matthew's and Luke's do, but John does tell us about the Word becoming flesh and coming into our world. In his prologue, we find these words:

> *He came to that which was his own, but his own did not receive him. Yet to all who did receive him, . . . he gave the right to become children of God.*
>
> *John 1:11-12 NIV*

These verses are sad and glorious at the same time. They are sad because they tell us that most of those Jesus "came to" rejected him. That was true not only at the time of Jesus' birth but also throughout his life. It is still true in our time. It is possible to ignore the signs, to be content with where we are, to be satisfied with what we have, and to think that more of the same is what we need when what we are longing for is something this world cannot provide.

Like the wondrous star that
guided the wise men to
the Christ child, God has
placed signs along your path,
all meant to lead you to him.

These verses are also glorious because they state that all who come to Jesus become the children of God. We come to know God through Christ the way a child knows a loving and tender father. We walk with God through life and find God to be a Father who cares deeply about us and provides guidance and protection. Because of Jesus, we can have a real, personal relationship with God. That's why Jesus came into the world and was born. Whether or not you realize it, your heart is not looking for a "something." You are longing for a Someone—Someone who knows you and loves you and gives you rest. Someone who can transform you and who will never leave you. That Someone is Jesus.

Like the wondrous star that guided the wise men to the Christ child, God has placed signs along your path, all meant to lead you to God. Are you ready to receive—whether for the first time or in a deeper and more meaningful way—the One the star foretold, the One you were created to know, the One who can give you peace, the One who offers himself in Jesus? If so, then humble your heart, ask to be forgiven of your sins, let God take his rightful place on the throne of your life, and worship God.

REFLECT

In what ways have you sensed that you were made for something more? How would you describe the yearning within your soul?

_____

_____

_____

_____

_____

_____

_____

_____

_____

What signs are pointing you to God this Advent?

_____

_____

_____

_____

_____

_____

_____

_____

_____

What excuses are keeping you from following those signs
and drawing closer to Jesus? What are you afraid of?

_____

_____

_____

_____

_____

_____

_____

_____

_____

MEDITATE

Deep calls to deep
*   in the roar of your waterfalls;*
all your waves and breakers
*   have swept over me.*
*By day the L*ORD *directs his love,*
*   at night his song is with me—*
*   a prayer to the God of my life.*
*   Psalm 42:7-8 NIV*

After Jesus was born in Bethlehem in Judea, during the time of King Herod, Magi from the east came to Jerusalem and asked, "Where is the one who has been born king of the Jews? We saw his star when it rose and have come to worship him."

When King Herod heard this he was disturbed, and all Jerusalem with him. When he had called together all the people's chief priests and teachers of the law, he asked them where the Messiah was to be born. "In Bethlehem in Judea," they replied, "for this is what the prophet has written:

> *"'But you, Bethlehem, in the land of Judah,*
> *   are by no means least among the rulers*
> *   of Judah;*
> *for out of you will come a ruler*
> *   who will shepherd my people Israel.'"*

Then Herod called the Magi secretly and found out from them the exact time the star had appeared. He sent them to

Bethlehem and said, "Go and search carefully for the child. As soon as you find him, report to me, so that I too may go and worship him."

After they had heard the king, they went on their way, and the star they had seen when it rose went ahead of them until it stopped over the place where the child was. When they saw the star, they were overjoyed. On coming to the house, they saw the child with his mother Mary, and they bowed down and worshiped him. Then they opened their treasures and presented him with gifts of gold, frankincense and myrrh. And having been warned in a dream not to go back to Herod, they returned to their country by another route.

Matthew 2:1-12 NIV

For to us a child is born,
to us a child is given, . . .
And he will be called
Wonderful Counselor, Mighty God,
Everlasting Father, Prince of Peace
Isaiah 9:6 NIV

PRAY

Heavenly Father, you have put a longing within my soul for something more than this world can provide—for Someone who can meet my every need and love me completely. That Someone is you. Thank you for giving me so many signs that lead me to you. Forgive me for making excuses and allowing fear of change—of the unknown—to keep me from pursuing you with all my heart. Give me a renewed sense of wonder this Christmas so that I will have the eyes to see you and all you are doing to reveal yourself to me. Thank you for the precious gift of your Son, Jesus, who points me to you. Amen.

ADVENT WREATH READING
THE FIRST SUNDAY OF ADVENT

Christmas Story Element: Star

Theme: Hope

Scripture: Isaiah 60:1-5

Light the Wreath:

In anticipation of the coming Christ, light the first candle of your Advent wreath.

Reflect:

Today we celebrate the wonder of the season like children on Christmas morning—with eyes wide open and hearts full of hope. And like Jesus, we say, "Let the children come to me, for the Kingdom of God belongs to them" (Matthew 19:14, author's paraphrase). We celebrate the wonder of the star placed high above Bethlehem, sent as a sign from God to announce the fulfillment of our deepest hopes and dreams— the birth of Immanuel, God with us.

Today focus on the hope we have in knowing that Jesus is the answer for our deepest needs.

Pray:

God of hope, open our eyes to the gift of wonder this season and help us to limit those things that distract us so that we may focus on you. Amen.

2.

The Wonder of a Name

2.

The Wonder of a Name

ED ROBB

*"She will bear a Son; and you shall call His name
Jesus, for He will save His people from their sins."*
Matthew 1:21 NASB

About this time of year, the world is reminded of the true
meaning of Christmas—that two thousand years ago a baby
boy was born to a Jewish couple in the town of Bethlehem.
Across the globe this holiday season, people will pull out

their Bibles to read the Christmas story. Those Bibles will have many different conditions—some may be covered with dust and filled with crisp, hardly-touched pages; others may have pages that are bent and battered, full of highlighted passages and notes written in the margins.

I hear many stories of families who have a special seasonal routine, a Christmas tradition that goes back generations. The tradition often involves family members sitting by the fire or beside the tree—with the smell of gingerbread cookies and the scent of fresh pine in the air—singing those old familiar Christmas carols before they read again the story of a baby born to change the world.

Others who did not grow up in the Christian faith may be opening a Bible for the first time, curious what all the fuss is over this Christ who lends his title to the term *Christmas*. Like many throughout history, they're seeking a hope to carry on.

Regardless of the scenario, when we take time to gaze into the birth narrative, there is one thing that may surprise us: two of the four Gospels are silent on the subject. Mark and John say *nothing* about the birth of Jesus.

Mark opens his Gospel not at an inn in Bethlehem but at a river in Galilee. Jesus is not in the crib but in the water being baptized. Mark skips all that nativity stuff and gets right to the action. That is his style: straightforward and vigorous, with an emphasis on what Jesus *did* rather than on his birth or even his words and teachings. Likewise, John leaves out the Christmas story, beginning his Gospel account with a strong dose of theology. He goes back, *not* to the mystery of that starlit night in Judea some two thousand years ago, but to the mystery of the Godhead before time began.

We have Matthew and Luke alone to thank for the Christmas story. They begin their stories with Jesus appearing not as a strong and fearless prophet but as a weak and helpless child. These two inspired writers give us the details of the birth of Christ. But it is interesting to note how much they vary—not in facts but in emphasis.

Luke, for example, tells the story from Mary's point of view, whereas Matthew tells us Joseph's side of the story. The more we know about Luke and Matthew, the more understandable this difference is.

Luke was a Gentile physician. In fact, he was the only Gentile of the New Testament authors. And so Luke carefully traces Jesus' lineage all the way back to Adam, the father of all of humanity. Luke stresses the universality of Christ and our Lord's special concern for the down-and-out and for women. It is in Luke's Gospel that we read of Elizabeth, Anna, and the woman who anointed Jesus' feet, wiping them with her tears and her hair. Knowing these details helps us to understand why Luke tells the story from Mary's point of view. He wants his readers to know that Jesus is for everyone, so he emphasizes his humble birth in a manger and tells of lowly shepherds coming to pay homage.

Matthew, on the other hand, was a Jewish patriot and tax collector. Though he also provides a list of Jesus' ancestors, he goes back only as far as Abraham, the father of the Jews. Matthew demonstrates that Christ is indeed the long-awaited Messiah, the one who will redeem captive Israel. He shows that all the evidence "adds up"—that the Old Testament prophecies are indeed fulfilled in Jesus.

It is important for us to remember that Jewish culture at that time was male-oriented and women were not highly esteemed. Everyday, in their morning prayers, male Jews would thank God that God did not make them a Gentile, a slave, or a woman. Women were not even allowed in the Temple. Knowing this helps us to understand why Matthew tells the story from Joseph's point of view, pictures Christ as the King of Israel, describes the wise men coming to pay homage, and tells about King Herod being so threatened that he tries to find and kill the newborn child.

Matthew and Luke weave the same tale from a different angle—one that is complimentary, not contradictory. Yet there is one point at which they converge—one detail that they both include: *the name of the child.*

What can we learn about this name that can help to awaken us to the wonder of Christmas?

A Special Name

Luke tells of the angel's announcement to Mary while Matthew tells of the angel's announcement to Joseph, yet in each instance the angel instructs them to name the child Jesus. In Matthew 1:21 we read, "You shall call His name Jesus," and in Luke 1:31 the angels says, "You shall name Him Jesus" (NASB). This detail seems rather important—important enough for God's messenger to tell both parents, and important enough for both Gospel writers to record it.

But why is it so important? Why is Jesus such a special name?

It's interesting considering the importance of a name at Christmastime. If there's one thing most of the world knows about the holiday, it's that gifts are given and received. When a person first enters the world as a baby, the first thing he or she is given—other than a rude awakening—is a name.

More often than not, the givers of that name—our parents—have thought long and hard about what to call us. There often is special meaning associated with the name we are given. Family history tends to play a big part in many parents' decisions. I know it did with my first child, but maybe not in the way you might think.

I'll never forget when he was born. The simple fact that my wife, Bev, gave birth to a boy caused all sorts of problems. You see, I was under intense family pressure to keep a family tradition going and name the little fellow Edmund W. Robb IV. To Bev, that seemed a bit much—almost arrogant. She said it sounded like what kings do. What were we trying to prove? Besides, what would we call the poor little fellow—Edmund? That didn't seem like a suitable name for a baby.

Back in those days, new mothers weren't rushed out of the hospital by insurance companies. For a couple of days we couldn't decide what to name our new baby. But after two days, the nurse came into our room and announced, "The doctor is releasing you this afternoon, but you can't go home until you give us a name for the birth certificate. So what is it?"

Bev looked at me and said, "Well, I suppose we had better keep family tradition." So Edmund Whetstone Robb IV it was.

The angel prevented that kind of domestic struggle for Mary and Joseph! He told them both to name the child Jesus.

Names are how we are identified. At the time that Bev and I were having children, the baby's gender was always a surprise, hidden until the moment of birth. Parents didn't know whether to decorate the newborn baby's room for a girl or boy. Baby showers often were held after the birth so that friends would know whether to buy for a girl or a boy. But once the use of ultrasound technology became routine, the infant's gender could be known early on in the pregnancy. With that surprise eliminated, many parents today choose to keep the baby's name secret until birth in order to have something to reveal.

The process of selecting a name also has changed since we had our children. Many parents today search the Internet, browsing baby name websites for a distinctive, unusual name. Then, invariably, when the child enrolls in preschool, they discover they were not the only new parents who chose that unique name. *How could there be several other children in the class with the same name?* many parents may wonder. Today names are almost a fashion statement for some, but it has not always been that way—especially not for the ancient Hebrews. For them, names held great meaning.

This is why we read in the Bible of names being changed to signify some new meaning. When God gave someone a new name, it was because a divine purpose was revealed to and placed within that person. Names connote identity in the biblical context; so a name change signified that God had transformed that person's identity and rerouted the trajectory of his or her life. The name became symbolic of the person's God-ordained mission to be an ambassador, a representative, and a living vessel of his grace, goodness, love, and hope in the world.

God changed Abram's name to Abraham, for example, as a sign of his promise that Abraham would become the father of many nations (Genesis 17:5). Likewise, Jesus changed Simon's name to Peter (Petros) because he said essentially, "You're going to be my rock" (see John 1:42 and Matthew 16:18). Throughout the Bible we see that names hold meaning, and this is certainly true in the Christmas story.

Joseph and Mary made the long journey to Nazareth, and when they arrived, Mary went into labor. Did this catch them by surprise? Was the baby coming early, perhaps because of the difficult trip? Neither Matthew's nor Luke's account tells us. Certainly the birth was on time according to divine schedule. This child of the most high was born exactly when and where God intended—in the city of David, just as ancient Scripture had promised (see Micah 5:2). Whether or not Mary or Joseph had settled on a name of their own liking is of no account, for as we've seen, the angel announced, "You shall call His name Jesus" (Matthew 1:21 NASB).

Why *Jesus*? What's so special about that name? Plenty. You see, Jesus is the Greek form of the Hebrew name Joshua, and that name meant something to Joseph and Mary. In fact, it meant something to every Jew, because it was the name of Moses' successor, Joshua.

Born into slavery in Egypt, Joshua was given the Hebrew name Hoshea, meaning salvation.[1] Being a slave, his name conveyed a hope, not a reality—at least not until many years later.

After living in slavery in Egypt, Hoshea and the other Hebrew slaves followed Moses out of bondage, across the Red Sea, and into the wilderness where they spent the next forty years wandering. Then Moses chose twelve men, one from each tribe, to cross the Jordan River and enter the Promised Land to spy out the country and bring back a report. Hoshea was one of the twelve. After returning forty days later, ten of the spies gave this report:

> *We went into the land to which you sent us, and it does flow with milk and honey! Here is its fruit. But the people who live there are*

> *powerful, and the cities are fortified and very*
> *large.... And they spread among the Israelites*
> *a bad report about the land they had*
> *explored. They said, "The land we explored*
> *devours those living in it. All the people we*
> *saw there are of great size."*
>
> *Numbers 13:27–28, 32 NIV*

But two of the spies, Caleb and Hoshea, tore their clothes in sorrow and said,

> *"The land we passed through and explored is*
> *exceedingly good. If the LORD is pleased with*
> *us, he will lead us into that land ... and will*
> *give it to us. Only do not rebel against the*
> *LORD. And do not be afraid of the people of*
> *the land.... the LORD is with us."*
>
> *Numbers 14:7–9 NIV*

We read in Numbers 13:16 that, even before sending the spies to explore the land, Moses changed Hoshea's name. He took two words—Jehovah (Yahweh), the proper name of the God of Israel,[2] and Hoshea, meaning salvation—and wove them together to form a new name, Joshua (Yehoshua in Hebrew), meaning "the Lord is salvation,"[3] or God saves. When Moses died, it was Joshua whom God chose as their leader. He is the one who led them out of the wilderness and into the Promised Land.

Through Joshua, God saved their people from a life of futility and death in the wilderness and brought them into the land of the living, a land flowing with milk and honey; a land of hope and promise; a land that would become the center of God's grace. Through the leadership of this man whose name means "The Lord is Salvation," Israel became a light for the world, a vine planted by God in the soil of the Middle East, destined by God to bring life to the nations.

When the angel announced to Joseph, "You shall call His name Jesus, for He will save His people from their sins" (Matthew 1:21 NASB), he was clearly communicating the reality of One who brings salvation to God's people once again—but in a way and manner that no ordinary human being could ever do. This time the One who bears the name meaning "the Lord is salvation" is actually the Lord of Salvation in the flesh, who had come to lead God's people out of a life of futility and death into the land of the living.

But this land of the living is not within the physical realm. No, it is a land that transcends this world we know and goes beyond time or space; it is otherworldly—heavenly! The Promised Land that Jesus came to usher us into is the kingdom of God, which has no end; it is eternal. That's why God sent Jesus—to lead us out of the wilderness of sin, sorrow, heartache, and emptiness into the Promised Land of his eternal presence.

A Name That Saves

Have you ever reflected on the fact that God sent his only Son into a mean and hostile world? Why would God do that? There had to be a problem that warranted such a plan. So what was the problem?

God knows that we need
more than a teacher, a healer,
a counselor, or a prophet.
We need a Savior. So he
sent Jesus. And that truly is
good news of great joy!

The problem could have been ignorance. People didn't understand who God was or what God expected. But if ignorance was the reason for sending Jesus, then he could have been a teacher and nothing more.

Perhaps the problem was our brokenness. God knows we're all broken and hurting inside. But if brokenness was the reason for sending Jesus, then he could have come as a healer and nothing more.

Maybe the problem was relational—our inability to get along with one another, even the people we love. But if relationships were the reason for sending Jesus, then he could have come as a counselor and nothing more.

Or perhaps the problem was poverty. But if that was the reason for sending Jesus, then he could have come as a prophet crying for economic justice or a financial advisor.

No, the problem went much deeper than ignorance, brokenness, relationships, or poverty.

The angel said to Joseph, "You shall call His name Jesus, for He will save His people from their sins" (Matthew 1:21 NASB). Likewise, the angel said to the shepherds: "Do not be afraid, for behold, I bring you good tidings of great joy which will be to all people. For there is born to you this day in the city of David a Savior, who is Christ the Lord" (Luke 2:10-11 NKJV).

God knows that we need more than a teacher, a healer, a counselor, or a prophet. We need a Savior. So God sent Jesus. And that truly is good news of great joy!

It is the good news that God loves you and wants a relationship with you. It is the good news that, no matter what you've done, God is not against you but for you. No matter how far you've wandered, God wants you back. Jesus said, "God did not send his Son into the world to condemn the world, but to save the world through him" (John 3:17 NIV).

Here's the reality. We all push God out of our lives. At some point we all reject the kind of relationship that God wants with us. At times some of us allow personal ambition to get in the way of our ambition for the kingdom.

Just the other day, I spoke with a young man I knew from the time he was a teenager. When I first met him, he took his faith seriously and was outspoken about his relationship with Jesus. After graduating in the top of his high school class, he went off to college and then to one of the most prestigious law schools in the country. Now he works at a highly respected law firm.

Of course, I congratulated him on his accomplishments, and he thanked me in return; but when I asked him what church he was attending, he told me he hadn't been to church for years because he was just too busy and had too much to do. He said, "Pastor, I've got so many personal goals to attain that I don't have time for religion."

Unfortunately, this story is all too familiar. So many people place their personal goals above their personal relationship with God. They are seeking a kingdom of their own instead of seeking first the kingdom of God. They are neglecting and rejecting the call that Jesus offers to each one of us when he says, "Come to Me" (Matthew 11:28 NASB).

The Bible calls our rejection of God *sin*, and that's why Jesus came. God knows that *all* of us need a Savior. Scripture says, "For all have sinned and fall short of the glory of God" (Romans 3:23 NIV). And God knows that we all need someone to lead us into the land of the living, or what Jesus refers to in John 10:10 as abundant life!

Sin is not a word we use much today, not even in the church. It sounds so out of touch with what we know today from the study of psychology—the fact that many of our wrong actions come from past wounds and hurts. The notion of sin doesn't fly well in a society that so often denies personal responsibility and believes nothing is truly wrong if it makes you feel good. But the Bible says we *all* are sinners and need a Savior.

The angel announced that Jesus would save his people from their sins. Who are "his people"? The Bible makes this clear for all to see. His people are those who believe on him and crown him Lord of Lords and Lord of their lives, as Paul so eloquently expresses in Philippians 2:9-11. "His people" is a statement that extends over the boundary line of Judaism to include the wise men who came from afar as well as the shepherds who tended sheep on Bethlehem's plains.

It includes *you* as well, if you'll let it. Jesus came to save you from sin and death so that you might experience the

Source of all life, so that you might live in the fullness of his grace and walk in the power of the Holy Spirit, so that you might reflect his light to those whose lives are filled with darkness, and so that you might be the hands and feet of Christ—loving and inviting others into the new Promised Land, which is the kingdom of God.

A New Name

My father grew up in the little town of Marshall in the piney woods of East Texas during the Great Depression. Times were hard. And in those days, entertainment was scarce. People made their own fun. But one form of entertainment they had was baseball. And so Marshall, like many smaller towns, had a semiprofessional baseball team. My dad's father worked for the railroad—an ordinary blue-collar job—but he was a star pitcher on the Marshall, Texas, semipro baseball team, and that made him somebody in that little town.

Because his dad was the pitcher, my father was able to go to the games for free. Well, one Saturday afternoon when he was about nine years old, he was walking through the gate on the way to the stands when he heard a voice bark, "Where do you think you're going, boy?"

Dad looked back, and it was a ticket taker at the gate. Dad said, "I'm going to the ball game."

"Not without a ticket, you ain't. Get out of here," the man growled.

Once you accept God's Christmas gift to the world and say yes to Jesus and the Savior's love, God gives you a new name: Christian. That name means Christ-follower, which indicates that you are God's precious child.

My dad went out and sat down on the running board of a car and cried. After a while, his father came along and asked, "What's wrong, son? Why are you crying?"

After hearing what had happened, his father said, "You just come with me, son." They walked over to the gate and his father said, "This is my boy."

At that, the ticket taker said, "Why, young man, why didn't you tell me you were Edmund Robb's son? You can come into this ballpark anytime you want to."

Names mean something! God has given you a new name—the highest name anyone can bear. Once you accept God's Christmas gift to the world and say yes to Jesus and the Savior's love, God gives you a new name: Christian. That name means Christ-follower, which indicates that you are God's precious child. It means you have accepted his gracious gift of salvation. It means you've got an everlasting ticket into his ballpark. It cost God an only Son, Jesus, who gave his life on the cross. But for you, it's free.

In his Gospel, John tell us:

> *The true light that gives light to everyone was coming into the world. He was in the world, and though the world was made through him, the world did not recognize him. He came to that which was his own, but his own did not receive him. Yet to all who did receive him, to those who believed in his name, he gave the*

> *right to become children of God—children*
> *born not of natural descent, nor of human*
> *decision or a husband's will, but born of God.*
>
> *John 1:9-13 NIV*

Will you come and experience the richness of his name? Will you invite Jesus, the Lord of Salvation, into your life to be both your Savior and your King? Will you take time to kneel before the manger this Christmas, submitting to his Lordship? Will you allow him to take first place in your life—not just during Christmas but throughout the days and years to come? Will you allow him to save you from your sin, guilt, and shame and be Lord of your time, talents, thoughts, resources, and plans? Will you bow before the King of kings and bask in his saving grace?

Multitudes from every age, nation, and tongue have already done this. They've come to him in faith, singing praises to his name. Why? Because they know what his name means for them personally: *Jehovah Hoshea*, God saves.

Christ is coming this Christmas so that you can experience the majesty of this name that was registered in heaven, delivered by an angel, and given to a newborn child—God's own Son, our Savior. You have the opportunity to welcome the birth of this gift of salvation again this year. My prayer is that you will receive this gift of God with great appreciation, expectation, and unspeakable joy.

REFLECT

What does the name Jesus mean to you personally?

_____

_____

_____

_____

_____

_____

_____

_____

_____

_____

How does understanding the meaning of Jesus' name impact your understanding or appreciation for what he came to do? In what ways has Jesus saved you?

_____

_____

_____

_____

_____

_____

_____

_____

_____

_____

What does the new name Christian—or Christ-follower—
reveal about you? How would you describe what the precious
gift of salvation means to you personally?

_____

_____

_____

_____

_____

_____

_____

_____

_____

MEDITATE

"Therefore the Lord Himself will give you a sign: Behold, a virgin will be with child and bear a son, and she will call His name Immanuel."

Isaiah 7:14 NASB

Now the birth of Jesus Christ was as follows: when His mother Mary had been betrothed to Joseph, before they came together she was found to be with child by the Holy Spirit. And Joseph her husband, being a righteous man and not wanting to disgrace her, planned to send her away secretly. But when he had considered this, behold, an angel of the Lord appeared to him in a dream, saying, "Joseph, son of David, do not be afraid to take Mary as your wife; for the Child who has been conceived in her is of the Holy Spirit. She will bear a Son; and you shall call His name Jesus, for He will save His people from their sins." Now all this took place to fulfill what was spoken by the Lord through the prophet: "BEHOLD, THE VIRGIN SHALL BE WITH CHILD AND SHALL BEAR A SON, AND THEY SHALL CALL HIS NAME IMMANUEL," which translated means, "GOD WITH US." And Joseph awoke from his sleep and did as the angel of the Lord commanded him, and took Mary as his wife, but kept her a virgin until she gave birth to a Son; and he called His name Jesus.

Matthew 1:18-25 NASB

Now in the sixth month the angel Gabriel was sent from God to a city in Galilee called Nazareth, to a virgin engaged to a man whose name was Joseph, of the descendants of David; and the virgin's name was Mary. And coming in, he said to her, "Greetings, favored one! The Lord is with you." But she was very perplexed at this statement, and kept pondering what kind of salutation this was. The angel said to her, "Do not be afraid, Mary; for you have found favor with God. And behold, you will conceive in your womb and bear a son, and you shall name Him Jesus. He will be great and will be called the Son of the Most High; and the Lord God will give Him the throne of His father David; and He will reign over the house of Jacob forever, and His kingdom will have no end."

Luke 1:26-33 NASB

In the same region there were some shepherds staying out in the fields and keeping watch over their flock by night. And an angel of the Lord suddenly stood before them, and the glory of the Lord shone around them; and they were terribly frightened. But the angel said to them, "Do not be afraid; for behold, I bring you good news of great joy which will be for all the people; for today in the city of David there has been born for you a Savior, who is Christ the Lord. This will be a sign for you: you will find a baby wrapped in cloths and lying in a manger." And suddenly there appeared with the angel a multitude of the heavenly host praising God and saying,

> *"Glory to God in the highest,*
> *And on earth peace among men with whom*
> *He is pleased."*

Luke 2:8-14 NASB

"For God so loved the world, that He gave His only begotten Son, that whoever believes in Him shall not perish, but have eternal life. For God did not send the Son into the world to judge the world, but that the world might be saved through Him.

John 3:16-17 NASB

PRAY

Jesus, your name is beautiful and special. You are the Lord of salvation—our God who saves. I am so grateful that you entered this hostile world to save us—to save me. You are so much more than a teacher, a healer, a counselor, and a prophet; you are our Savior! And that is good news! May the wonder of your name fill my heart with joy this Christmas and always. In your precious name I pray. Amen.

ADVENT WREATH READING
THE SECOND SUNDAY OF ADVENT

Christmas Story Element: Name

Theme: Peace

Scripture: Matthew 1:18-21

Light the Wreath:

In anticipation of the coming Christ, light the second candle in your Advent wreath; then light the first candle you lit last week.

Reflect:

Today, like Mary, we wait for the Christ child. We celebrate all that God has already done and say, "My soul glorifies the Lord / and my spirit rejoices in God my Savior" (Luke 1:46-47 NRSV). We reflect on the wonder of the precious name of Jesus, our Savior and Prince of Peace.

Today, focus on the peace that comes from knowing that Jesus is the God who saves.

Pray:

God of peace, help us to remember that you have come to save us and fill us with your peace as we trust in your mighty name. Amen.

3.

The Wonder of a Manger

3.

The Wonder
of a Manger

ED ROBB

"And she brought forth her firstborn son, and wrapped him in swaddling clothes, and laid him in a manger; because there was no room for them in the inn."

Luke 2:7 KJV

Christmas means different things to different people. To some the wonder of Christmas is about bright lights and Christmas trees. To others it is about gathering with family and friends and exchanging presents. But for those of us who follow Jesus, the wonder of Christmas is about the birth of our Savior. And so at Christmas, we focus on the nativity scene and the manger that held the precious Christ child.

There is one nativity and manger that I will never forget. It was Christmastime during the fall of my freshman year in college. The Methodist Missions agency had come to the small Christian campus where I attended—Asbury College in Wilmore, Kentucky—for a conference, and they brought a life-size nativity scene as part of a display that had been handcrafted by an African tribe. Though I don't know why, for some reason my roommate and I decided to steal baby Jesus. I'll never forget when a school official showed up at our room the next night. He had been told that we were the culprits, and he wanted baby Jesus back—and he meant *now*.

My roommate looked him straight in the eyes and said, "No sir, we did not do it. I have no idea what you're talking about." I was shocked, because I was about to confess and plead for mercy. For some reason, I wasn't asked, and I felt no reason to contradict my roommate's testimony.

We knew we had to get rid of the evidence, but you just can't toss baby Jesus in the lake or the dumpster. Thieves, yes, but hardened sinners, no. We couldn't do that! So the next night, the two of us snuck back into the foyer of the

Conference Center (thankfully, there were no security cameras back then) and put the baby Jesus back in the manger.

That's probably not the first story you've ever heard about someone stealing baby Jesus from the manger. It seems to be a common prank at Christmastime. What's surprising to me is not that someone would steal baby Jesus from the manger but that anyone would put him in a manger in the first place.

What is the wonder of a manger? What can we learn from this unlikely crib that can help to awaken us to the wonder of Christmas?

An Unlikely Crib

We tend to romanticize the manger, decorating our homes and churches with nativity scenes. My wife, Bev, collects them. We must have a dozen that we place around the house as part of our Christmas decorations—and another dozen that remain in boxes in the attic. You see, Bev has so many nativities that some are displayed only every few years on a rotating basis. But the truth is that there was nothing romantic about Jesus' birth.

Luke's Gospel gives us the details leading up to the birth. Two parents traveled to the small town of Bethlehem, which was far from their home in Nazareth. There was no hospital, no birthing center, and likely no midwife to assist. Their journey to Bethlehem began when Caesar Augustus decreed that "all the world should be taxed . . . every one into his own city" (Luke 2:1-3 KJV). Bethlehem was the hometown of Joseph's ancestors, so they made their way there. Soon after their arrival, Mary went into labor, but there was no room to be found anywhere. With so many pilgrims in town, all the inns were full—sold out.

My wife, Bev, and I had an all-too-similar experience when Bev was pregnant with our daughter, Ashley. We were traveling to California for a conference on Labor Day weekend. It was our first trip to California, so we decided to drive down Highway 1. Perhaps you have experienced this road that hugs the Pacific coastline. It is one of the most scenic highways in the world.

Some friends had told us, "Oh, you must stay in the Highlands Inn, just outside Carmel. It's charming. You will love it."

So we went. Not realizing that a reservation was advisable, we simply showed up. And we were told, "Sorry, there's no room. It's Labor Day weekend, and we are completely full." We told ourselves that Highlands Inn looked too expensive for us anyway, and so we put Plan B into action and began to look for another hotel. But there were no vacancies to be found anywhere. As it neared midnight and our search continued, I started sending Bev to the reception desk alone, thinking that the sight of her might help. After all, she was "great with child"!

Still we were turned away, one motel after another. Finally we gave up and drove south on Highway 1 until we reached a roadside park next to the Pacific Ocean. We pulled over and slept in the car! Let's just say that we could sympathize with Mary and Joseph, finding no room in the inn.

Scripture tells us that baby Jesus was laid in a manger because there was no room for them in the inn (Luke 2:7). The original Greek word was *kataluma*, which can be translated as "inn" or "guest room."[1] Tradition suggests that baby Jesus was born in a stable—perhaps out back behind an inn. Contemporary theologians have suggested that it also was possible he was born beneath or outside the guest quarters of a very crowded house. Because more vulnerable animals were often brought in at night for protection, a feeding trough or manger would have been nearby.[2] In either case, the circumstances certainly were not ideal for the birth of a baby.

At Christmas we often sing these familiar words,

> Away in a manger, no crib for a bed,
> the little Lord Jesus laid down his sweet
> head

Though we sing that carol with a romanticized notion, it certainly was not a romantic experience for Mary and Joseph. After all, they laid their child in a *manger*—a feeding trough for the animals. "How could we have let this happen?" they must have been asking themselves.

How *did* it happen? This was the Christ Child, God's own Son sent from above, the Savior of the world. If God was in charge—and God was—how did God allow this to happen? Did some angel, perhaps Gabriel, forget to make the reservation? As I've said, what's surprising to me is that anyone would put Jesus in a manger in the first place—especially God. For Mary and Joseph, everything—the humble birth, the manger, the animals, the shepherds barging in—was a most unfortunate accident. But to God, it was by design. The location and circumstances of Jesus' birth had been divinely orchestrated. Why, then, would God do this to his only begotten Son?

God wanted the world to know the nature of Jesus' reign from the beginning. The manger was a harbinger of Christ's entire ministry. It spoke volumes about the way the Sovereign Ruler of the universe intended to win back God's lost children—not by overwhelming us with might but winning us with love.

For God, it was never a matter of power. God never intended to force or scare us back into relationship. If all God desired was our submission, this could have been accomplished rather easily—and quickly. But God desired far more than submission; God wanted an authentic relationship with us. And God was willing to go to any length for that to happen.

Throughout Scripture, God is revealed as a seeker. We find God on a continual pursuit for something. We find the Father seeking (John 4:23), scanning the earth from heaven (Psalm 14:2), God's eyes running to and fro throughout the

The manger was a harbinger
of Christ's entire ministry.
It spoke volumes about the
way the Sovereign Ruler of
the universe intended to win
back his lost children—not by
overwhelming us with might
but winning us with love.

---

planet to find something (2 Chronicles 16:9). We find Jesus telling us that he has come to seek (Luke 19:10). He gives us a deeper glimpse into his heart by comparing himself with a shepherd who leaves ninety-nine sheep to seek the one lost (Luke 15:4–7), with a woman combing through her entire house on the search for a lost coin (Luke 15:8–10), with a father who incessantly scans the horizon for the return of the prodigal son (Luke 15:20), and with a merchant seeking fine pearls (Matthew 13:45-46).

Benjamin Schäfer, a self-described blog theologian, writes,

> Throughout Scripture we encounter a God who is on a quest, a seeking God, chasing and pursuing. The pages of the Bible are permeated with the seeking of God. God has been a seeker all along. It's within His nature, it's who He is and something He enjoys about Himself. Yet it should startle us that the completely omniscient, self-sufficient God that owns everything and needs nothing would seek for something, and that this something would be us.[3]

Oh, the wonder of a manger—that God would set aside God's deity and enter the stream of human history as a vulnerable child in order to bring us back into relationship.

As Charles Wesley wrote in the great hymn "And Can It Be that I Should Gain,"

He left His Father's throne above
(so free, so infinite his grace!),
emptied himself of all but love,
and bled for Adam's helpless race.
'Tis mercy all, immense and free;
for, O my God, it found out me![4]

A Quiet Invasion

From the moment Adam and Eve rebelled against God's divine rule and humanity fell into sin, God the Father began the plan to win us back—to deliver us from evil and save us from our self-destruction. And God began the divine act of redemption by choosing a people to whom God would reveal God's character and truth over the centuries—through prophets and sages; through powerful experiences of saving grace, such as when God sent Moses to rescue God's chosen people from slavery in Egypt; and through Holy Scripture. Then, when the right time came, God personally stepped into our world—Emmanuel, God with us.

In his book *Abundant Living*, the great missionary E. Stanley Jones told the story of a little boy at a mission boarding school during World War II. Because of the fighting, the little fellow couldn't get home for the holidays. So when Christmas Day came, the little boy was terribly sad and nothing could cheer him. When he didn't come out of his room for dinner, the headmaster went to check on him. Trying to console the young boy, the principal asked what he would like for Christmas. The little guy looked at a photograph of his dad, which stood on his dresser, and with tears in his eyes he said wistfully, "I wish father would step out of the picture."[5]

That's what happened at Bethlehem on that starlit Christmas night. Christ, the Son, stepped out of eternity, put on human flesh, and entered our world. I like the way William Ezell describes it: "It is as though we were looking at God through one of those snowy glass balls and couldn't clearly see God, so Jesus stepped out of the encasement and took up residence on this planet so we could better understand and know God."[6]

The Creator of the universe took on human flesh. The Apostle John describes it like this in his Gospel: "The Word became flesh and made his dwelling among us" (John 1:14 NIV). Theologians call this the Incarnation. Jesus, being fully God and having a fully divine nature, became fully human, possessing a body and living in space and time just as we do.

Jesus is human in every way except for the reality that he was without sin. He had human senses. He looked upon people with compassion. He laid hands upon them, touching the lame and the blind. He heard the cries for mercy from those who were afflicted with emotional, psychological, spiritual, or physical pain. He drank from the same cup and ate the same bread as his disciples. Jesus experienced heartbreak and cried with Mary over the memory of her dead brother, Lazarus. Jesus laughed with his friends and felt the heartbreak of betrayal, denial, and abandonment. Jesus was fully human and fully God. This means that in his humanity he can empathize with our experiences, good or bad; at the same time, he can bring divine healing and comfort.

The wonder of a manger is that God's Son humbled himself and came to earth to save us from sin and, as we read in 1 John, "to destroy the works of the devil" (1 John 3:8 NASB). Yet it was a quiet invasion—not at all the way one might have expected.

One summer, Bev and I traveled to Normandy, France. We spent an entire day touring the beaches and battlefields with a guide whose maternal grandparents had both been killed on D-Day when an Allied bomb missed its target and hit their cottage. Yet she didn't blame the Americans. "It was a tragic accident," she told us with tears in her eyes, "and it cost our family dearly, but your countrymen paid a tremendous price too."

Touring those beaches was a powerful and sobering experience, especially visiting the American Cemetery with its thousands of graves—most marked by simple white crosses.

D-day, which took place on June 6, 1944, was the largest seaborne invasion in history when some 156,000 American, British, and Canadian forces landed on five beaches along a fifty-mile stretch of the heavily fortified coast of France's Normandy region.[7] For hours, waves of American aircraft

With one word God could have
sent ten thousand angels and
overwhelmed this earth with his
omnipotent power. But he chose
a much different approach—a
sleepy, quiet approach…. Oh, the
wonder of a manger—that God
would quietly invade the world
and come to live among us.

---

had flown overhead, dropping powerful bombs to soften the enemy defenses.

Think of the deafening sound of those bombs exploding. Think of the horrific sound of the German artillery as desperate soldiers tried to shoot down Allied bombers and stop our advancing troops. It was a terrifying and shocking day. Thousands of sailors and soldiers lost their lives. But the Allies were utterly determined to rescue Europe from the dark and evil grip of Hitler and Nazism.

Compare that invasion to God's quiet invasion of this earth, which was so different—counterintuitive, even. Pastor Darrell Johnson has called it "the sleepy invasion." In a sermon by that title, he writes,

> The stage was set. It was finally the fullness of time. The world had long been in prison, caught in a web of sin and death, controlled by a network of forces and powers hostile to God and his people. God Almighty, King of the universe, Lord of history, the rightful Sovereign of the Earth, was about to invade this world. He was about to come and conquer the great enemies, sin and death, and to triumph over the powers of evil.[8]

With one word God could have sent ten thousand angels and overwhelmed this earth with his omnipotent power.

But he chose a much different approach—a sleepy, quiet approach. Johnson writes, "And the only sound you hear is the gentle breathing of a baby sleeping in his mother's arms. A baby. A baby. A baby."[9]

The angels praised God, but only the shepherds heard. A brilliant star shined over the Savior's birthplace, but it seems that only some wise men from the east followed it.

David J. Kalas writes,

> I call Christmas "God's sneak attack" because he didn't come into the world marching through the front door. He didn't come with power or prominence, with influence or importance. He didn't come into the spotlight. God came into the world through the back door. He snuck in.[10]

Oh, the wonder of a manger—that God would quietly invade the world and come to live among us; that Jesus would come not in power but in weakness; that Jesus would humble himself from the beginning, being born not in a palace but in lowly surroundings; that the newborn King would be encircled not by a royal entourage but by lowly shepherds.

Why would the Sovereign Lord of the universe do that? There is just one reason—because of God's great love for us. God wants to win our hearts and make us God's forever. God doesn't only receive those who come to God; God is even actively reaching out for us. Listen to God's own words from Jeremiah:

> *"I have loved you with an everlasting love;*
> *I have drawn you with unfailing*
> *kindness."*
>
> *Jeremiah 31:3 NIV*

A Divine Plan

Jesus' entrance into the world was not the way we would have imagined, but God's ways are always full of wonder. The location and circumstances of his birth were not an accident or a misstep by the Angel Gabriel or Joseph. Not at all! They were divinely orchestrated. God sent the only begotten Son in this humble way because God wanted us to know that Jesus' reign would be characterized by humility. You see, Jesus came to show us the way to live—to demonstrate from the very beginning that true greatness comes not by exalting yourself but by serving others.

As we follow the footsteps of Jesus in the Gospels, we see him reaching out to hurting and forgotten people. We see him putting others' needs ahead of his own. We see him believing the best in people. We see him bending down to touch the sick and the outcast and weeping at the heartbreak and loss of his friends. We see him putting on an apron and washing his disciples' feet. And finally, we see him giving his life on a cross for our sins, the sins of the world:

Jesus came to show us the way
to live—to demonstrate from
the very beginning that true
greatness comes not by exalting
yourself but by serving others.

> *For God was pleased to have all his fullness*
> *dwell in him, and through him to reconcile*
> *to himself all things, whether things on earth*
> *or things in heaven, by making peace through*
> *his blood, shed on the cross.*
>
> *Colossians 1:19–20 NIV*

Christ was determined to show us the secret of true happiness and the way to inner peace, both of which come only through obeying God and serving others. When you live in the stream of God's will, you are moving in sync with the universe. You're moving in tandem with the divine DNA God has placed within you. You find yourself in harmony with God's creative design, and life becomes balanced. Your soul beats in rhythm with God's heart, and you find contentment.

It was no accident that Jesus was born among the animals and placed in a manger. It was no accident that Jesus devoted himself to serving others. It was no accident that he confronted the dark forces of this world until he was nailed to a cross. That was the Savior's M.O. The Bible tells us that this child of Bethlehem is none other than the omnipotent God himself:

> *Though he was God,*
> * he did not think of equality with God*
> * as something to cling to.*

Instead, he gave up his divine privileges;
> *he took the humble position of a servant*
> *and was born as a human being.*

When he appeared in human form,
> *he humbled himself in obedience to God*
> *and died a criminal's death on a cross.*

Therefore, God elevated him to the place of highest honor
> *and gave him the name above all other names,*

that at the name of Jesus every knee should bow,
> *in heaven and on earth and under the earth,*

and every tongue declare that Jesus Christ is Lord,
> *to the glory of God the Father.*
>
> *Philippians 2:6-11 NLT*

Imagine with me that you are there beside the manger. It is a silent night, a Holy night, as we fall to our knees in wonder, beholding a tiny King. It is a silent night, a Holy night, as tiny hands reach out in wonder, beholding his precious Kingdom.

After the fall of the Iron Curtain, when communism came crashing down, the full extent of the evil that had scarred the environment and the people became apparent. An American named Will Fish volunteered to go to Moscow with another American and work with orphans who had been abused, abandoned, and left in the care of a government-run program. They share the story of a special Christmas they experienced while there in the article "A Russian Christmas Story: 'For Always.'"[11]

As the Christmas season was approaching, they prepared to share the traditional Christmas story with the orphans, who would be hearing it for the first time. They told them about Mary and Joseph traveling to Bethlehem and finding no room in the inn. They explained that Jesus was born in a stable and placed in a manger. The children and the workers of the orphanage sat attentively, listening with amazement.

When they finished telling the story, they gave each of the children three small pieces of cardboard and asked them to make a simple manger. They also gave each child a small square cut from a napkin for the baby Jesus. As Will walked among the children to see if they needed help, he came to a little boy name Misha, who appeared to about six years old. Noticing that Misha's manger had not one but two babies in it, he called for a translator to ask the boy about it.

Though he had heard the Christmas story just once, Misha accurately relayed what happened until he came to part where Mary put baby Jesus in the manger. Then he began to ad lib, saying:

> And when Maria laid the baby in the manger, Jesus looked at me and asked me if I had a place to stay. I told him I have no

mamma and I have no papa, so I don't have any place to stay. Then Jesus told me I could stay with him. But I told him I couldn't, because I didn't have a gift to give him like everybody else did. But I wanted to stay with Jesus so much, so I thought maybe if I kept him warm that would be a good gift. So I asked Jesus, "If I keep you warm, will that be a good enough gift?" And Jesus told me, "If you keep me warm, that will be the best gift anybody ever gave me." So I got into the manger and then Jesus looked at me and he told me I could stay with him—for always."[12]

As Misha finished, his eyes were brimming with tears that spilled down his cheeks. He covered his face with his hand, lowered his head to the table, and sobbed. Will concludes with these powerful words: "The little orphan had found someone who would never abandon nor abuse him, someone who would stay with him—for always."[13]

Oh, the wonder of a manger—that God's divine plan was to send a Son so that we might be with God forever. As Benjamin Schäfer, observed in his blog, "It's stunning how approachable God makes Himself. He is not hiding somewhere, concealing Himself from mankind. He hasn't made it difficult or complicated to find Him. It's not a special privilege reserved for only a few select. He wants to be found, He wants to be known."[14] God wants us to come to the manger.

What beautiful words: "And she brought forth her firstborn son, and wrapped him in swaddling clothes, and laid him in a manger; because there was no room for them in the inn" (Luke 2:7 KJV). What a wonderful, beautiful picture of God's love for you and for me.

REFLECT

What does the humble birth of the Christ-child reveal about God and God's plan?

_____

_____

_____

_____

_____

_____

_____

_____

How does thinking of Christmas as a "quiet invasion" or a "sneak attack" enrich your understanding of the meaning and significance of Christmas?

_____

_____

_____

_____

_____

_____

_____

_____

How would you describe what the wonder of the manger
means for you personally?

_____

_____

_____

_____

_____

_____

_____

_____

MEDITATE

Now in those days a decree went out from Caesar Augustus, that a census be taken of all the inhabited earth. This was the first census taken while Quirinius was governor of Syria. And everyone was on his way to register for the census, each to his own city. Joseph also went up from Galilee, from the city of Nazareth, to Judea, to the city of David which is called Bethlehem, because he was of the house and family of David, in order to register along with Mary, who was engaged to him, and was with child. While they were there, the days were completed for her to give birth. And she gave birth to her firstborn son; and she wrapped Him in cloths, and laid Him in a manger, because there was no room for them in the inn.

In the same region there were some shepherds staying out in the fields and keeping watch over their flock by night. And an angel of the Lord suddenly stood before them, and the glory of the Lord shone around them; and they were terribly frightened. But the angel said to them, "Do not be afraid; for behold, I bring you good news of great joy which will be for all the people; for today in the city of David there has been born for you a Savior, who is Christ the Lord. This will be a sign for you: you will find a baby wrapped in cloths and lying in a manger." And suddenly there appeared with the angel a multitude of the heavenly host praising God and saying,

"Glory to God in the highest,
And on earth peace among men with
whom He is pleased."

When the angels had gone away from them into heaven, the
shepherds began saying to one another, "Let us go straight to
Bethlehem then, and see this thing that has happened which
the Lord has made known to us." So they came in a hurry and
found their way to Mary and Joseph, and the baby as He lay
in the manger.

Luke 2:1-16 NASB

For God was pleased to have all his fullness dwell in him, and
through him to reconcile to himself all things, whether things
on earth or things in heaven, by making peace through his
blood, shed on the cross.

Colossians 1:19-20 NIV

Though he was God,
  he did not think of equality with God
  as something to cling to.
Instead, he gave up his divine privileges;
  he took the humble position of a slave
  and was born as a human being.
When he appeared in human form,
  he humbled himself in obedience to God
  and died a criminal's death on a cross.

Therefore, God elevated him to the place of highest honor
    and gave him the name above every name,
that at the name of Jesus every knee should bow,
    in heaven and on earth and under the earth,
and every tongue declare that Jesus Christ is Lord,
    to the glory of God the Father.

                    Philippians 2:6-11 NLT

PRAY

Lord Jesus, I stand in awe that you would humble yourself and come to earth to live among us—to love us, serve us, and fight on our behalf, being willing to give your very life so that we might truly live. How grateful I am for your surprising and wonderful divine plan! Open my eyes this season to the wonder of a manger—an unlikely crib that heralds your humble and eternal reign. May this beautiful picture of your love profoundly change me, and may I follow your example by humbling myself to love and serve others in your name. Amen.

ADVENT WREATH READING
THE THIRD SUNDAY OF ADVENT

Christmas Story Element: Manger

Theme: Love

Scripture: Luke 2:1-20

Light the Wreath:

In anticipation of the coming Christ, light the third candle in your Advent wreath; then light the other two candles you've lit previously.

Reflect:

Today, like the shepherds, we watch for signs of the Messiah's birth and celebrate the good news that was proclaimed for all people, saying, "Glory to God in the highest heaven, / and on earth peace to those on whom his favor rests" (Luke 2:14 NIV). We reflect on the wonder of the manger, which represents God's rescue mission to come and save us—his beloved children.

Today, focus on the love that sent Jesus to be born in a humble manger.

Pray:

God of love, help us to believe in and experience the extraordinary, never-ceasing love you have for us, and show us how we can share this wonderful love with others. Amen.

4.

The Wonder of
a Promise

4.

The Wonder of a Promise

ROB RENFROE

"Therefore the Lord himself will give you a sign. Look, the young woman is with child and shall bear a son, and shall name him Immanuel."

Isaiah 7:14 NRSV

Life can be confusing and the way dark. Sometimes it can be as dark as a winter's night, and often it feels just as cold. We can feel alone, thinking there is no one smiling on us, no one looking out for us, and no one who really understands who we are, what we are facing, or how we feel inside. Have you ever felt that way? We all have at one time or another.

Some of us feel alone; others of us live alone. And for some reason, our loneliness can be magnified at Christmas. Maybe it's the crowds that surround us, the reminder of loved ones we have lost, or the memory of Christmas as children when we believed anything was possible. Now those dreams are gone, and we just hope to make it through another day. Or maybe it's the time of the year. We step outside into the night, and it's dark, cold, and quiet—strangely quiet. The air is heavy, the sounds are muffled, and the only thing we can hear is our own heart beating.

There are many reasons why a baby named Jesus was born into our world, but one of the most important is so that we would never have to be alone—so that *you* would never have to face a dark night or a cold world or a lost cause on your own, because Someone is here for you. Someone who understands you, knows your fears, and remembers your sorrows. Someone who is committed to you. Someone who knew you before you knew yourself. No matter where you've wandered or what you've done, this Someone wants to walk through this world with you.

We've considered the wonder of a star, the wonder of a name, and the wonder of a manger. Each holds deep and rich meaning for us, yet all point us to the same thing: the wonder of a promise. God made a promise through the prophet Isaiah:

> *"The virgin will conceive a child! She will give*
> *birth to a son and will call him Immanuel*
> *(which means 'God is with us')."*
>
> *Isaiah 7:14 NLT*

The Old Testament reveals that God's people "believed in God." First and foremost, they believed in God *above us*. When they sinned, they believed in God *against us*. And when they thought they were doing everything right, they were able to believe in God *for us*. But they did not believe in God *with us*—at least not in the ways we need most. Not with us as a mother or father is with a child. Not with us as person who understands what it is like to be human—a tiny being in a monstrously large universe. Not with us as one who knows what it's like to give your best and see it do no good, to give your heart only to be rejected, or to cry at night because those you love are hurting and you can't take their pain away.

No, they couldn't believe that God is with us like that. So, aware of God's holiness and uncertain of the depth of his love, the Israelites always wanted there to be someone between themselves and God—Moses, a priest, a prophet, a king; someone who would intercede on their behalf and protect them. But God had a plan to be more than God *above us* or God *among us* or even God *for us*. The desire of God's heart was to be God *with us*—so that we would never have to be alone on Christmas or any other day of the year, from the best day to the worst.

So in the fullness of time, the wonder of God's promise came to pass! The virgin Mary was with child, and she gave birth and named the child Immanuel, God with us, just as the angel instructed. Jesus is God with us—not just God *among us*, living in the same world we live in yet untouched by its pain and brokenness, but God *with us*, experiencing life in the same ways that we do.

You are not alone. Jesus knows how you feel when your friends desert you, because his friends deserted him. He knows what it's like for your enemies to mock you, because his enemies mocked him. He knows what it's like when a loved one betrays you, because he was betrayed. He knows the pain of crying beside a loved one's grave when death has torn a chasm in your heart and you feel as if you're falling in, because he lost people he loved. He knows what it's like to be tempted, because he was tempted. He knows what it's like to struggle to do the Father's will, because he struggled even to the point of sweating blood. He knows what it's like to suffer, because he was bruised in body and in spirit. He even knows how hot is the breath and how cold are the fingers of death when the final hour comes.

That is the wonder of Christmas—the coming of God into our world in Jesus Christ as both the Lord of Creation and Immanuel—God with us. Let that sink in.

There is no promise more
wondrous, more empowering,
or more real than the promise of
Christmas. In Jesus Christ, God is
Immanuel, God with you today,
tomorrow, and forever.

Our God has scars—scars he received because he came to live in the same cruel world that we live in. Let life do to you what it will. Let life take your dreams, your health, your loved ones, and your ability to figure things out and make sense of it all. But don't ever let it take from you the certainty that God is with you and will never forsake you. You are never alone. If you hold on to that promise, it will be enough to see you through.

We exist by *fact*—what has happened to us and what is now happening around us. But we live, thrive, and overcome by *promise*. And there is no promise more wondrous, more empowering, or more real than the promise of Christmas. In Jesus Christ, God is Immanuel, God with you today, tomorrow, and forever.

Christmas is not only a promise we are meant to experience; it's a promise we are meant to keep. In other words, it's a promise we are meant to fulfill and make real in the lives of others. Once we come to faith in Jesus and the Holy Spirit comes into our lives, we are meant to be the presence of God in the lives of others, doing God's work and fulfilling God's promise to be with people who are confused, hurting, or lost.

That's one of the reasons the church is called the body of Christ, because we are in the world to do what Jesus did. Through us, those who are lost will know that God is Immanuel, God with them. We fulfill the promise and bring the presence of God into the lives of others the way that Jesus did.

Who were most open to Jesus when he walked the earth? Who fell in love with him and opened their lives to him more readily than anyone else? Those everyone thought had the most reason to feel guilty. Those the Pharisees referred to as "sinners." And in all likelihood, because they were defined that way and were looked down upon by their culture, that's how they thought of themselves. Why were they drawn to Jesus when he told them to repent and change their lives? Because when others rejected them, Jesus spent time with them. When others condemned them, Jesus comforted them. And when others said they deserved sickness and disease, Jesus healed their bodies and brought peace to their souls. When others stood against these individuals, Jesus stood for them. When others stood above them, Jesus stood with them. Because they knew he cared about them and was with them, they cared about what he had to say when he spoke truth into their lives.

Our world is lost, broken, confused, and angry. Our world is full of itself and empty of God. Much of our world hates the church and finds the gospel offensive. What are we to tell a lost, angry world with our words and our lives? We are to share the promise of Christmas, which for us has come to pass: "The virgin was with child and gave birth to a son, and he is called Immanuel—God with us" (Matthew 1:23, author's paraphrase). The way we tell that message and keep that promise is by being *with* people—not against them, above them, or among them but *with* them.

How can we do that? I'd like to suggest three ways.

What are we to tell a lost, angry world with our words and our lives? We are to share the promise of Christmas, which for us has come to pass [through Christ's coming].... The way we tell that message and keep that promise is by being with people—not against them, above them, or among them but with them.

We Must Understand the People We Want to Reach

One of the most important things we must understand is that all of us carry something: loss, hurt, or broken dreams; guilt, emptiness, or loneliness; the bad decision we are ashamed of, the fear we don't have what it takes, or the nagging suspicion that if people saw us for who we really are, we would end up alone and unloved. Each of us carries something—even those of us who follow Jesus. On top of that, we have the weight of the things our culture has promised us: salvation through technology, possessions, the pleasures of the flesh, or enough friends and followers on social media. But our culture has failed to keep its promises.

No doubt you have friends, coworkers, and family members who have experienced all this world has to offer yet are left wondering, *Is this all there is?* They are disappointed and confused, unfulfilled and disillusioned—not understanding how they can have everything yet still be without peace or contentment. Often those who are difficult to love—or even to like—are that way because they are hurting inside. And often those who are angry about religion have given up on God because they believe God has given up on them. Sometimes when life gets us down, we can find ourselves struggling with similar thoughts and emotions. Living in this world can be tough, yet we are called to share the hope we have with others.

What do we need to understand about the people we are meant to reach with the promise of Christmas—those we are to be with and to share the presence of God? We must understand that they have lost something important, something essential, and they don't know where to find it. That is a painful way to go through life, trying to hide from the pain within.

Jesus referred to those who needed him as sheep without a shepherd (Matthew 9:36 and Mark 6:34), those who labor and are heavy laden (Matthew 11:28), and those who are sick and in need of a doctor (Matthew 9:12, Mark 2:17, and Luke 5:31). Yes, he saw their sin. But more important, he saw their hearts and understood their struggle. He was with them in the hard and ugly places of their lives. And he is with us in the hard and ugly places of our lives as well.

If we are going to fulfill the promise of Immanuel and be Jesus' presence in the lives of others, we must understand that all of us carry something that makes us weary and hurts our heart. All of us need the promise of Christmas.

We Must Remember Our Own Stories

Something unfortunate can happen when God works in our lives—saving us from our sins, changing our hearts, and getting us to a better place. We can forget our own stories—how lost, desperate, confused, and hopeless we were, and how willing we were to do just about anything to make the pain go away. If we forget that part of our stories, then when we see people who are lost or angry or hurting, we can be tempted to say to ourselves, "What's wrong with them? I was hurting, but I found a way to make it through and to have joy. Why can't they do the same thing?" When we do that, we become hard and judgmental and unable to be *with* people in the way that Jesus was. It is my hope and prayer that we will never forget what we were like before we experienced the grace of God, because if we can remember that, we will feel concern and compassion for others and be able to be the presence of God in their lives.

I'm going to share an unflattering part of my own story that is important for me to remember with the hope that it will help you to remember difficult parts of your own story and then be able to show compassion for the stories of others.

Nearly thirty years ago some things happened in my personal life—my life outside the church—that I thought were unfair, manipulative, and controlling. And I became angry and bitter. As I look back on it, I recognize that my response was due to pride and selfishness. But at the time it was as if I had fallen into a black hole. My typically playful and friendly sarcasm gave way to dark cynicism. I masked it pretty well at church, but I didn't hold back at home. All of the darkness and meanness that had filled my soul spilled out onto my wife, Peggy, and our family. This went on not for a few days or weeks but for the better part of a year.

Peggy is so loving and caring, but she came to the point when she said, "Rob, is this ever going to change, or is this

If we are going to fulfill
the promise of Immanuel and
be Jesus' presence in the lives
of others, we must understand
that all of us carry something
that makes us weary and hurts
our heart. All of us need the
promise of Christmas.

who you're always going to be? Because I don't think I can live like this; I know I don't want to." True to where I was at the time, I said, "Fine, if you don't want to be here, you don't have to stay. If you think you can find someone else better, God bless you; I'm sure you can."

I'm not proud of that. It's still painful to remember, but that's where I was. That's where people can end up in life—far away from God and willing to sacrifice what they care about most on the altar of the ego because of their hurt and pride.

Do you want to know something ironic? At the very same time, I was leading the church's healing prayer ministry. That's right, I was praying for others and teaching people how to pray for those who are broken and hurting physically, emotionally, and spiritually. It was because of that role that Peggy and I went to California to attend a conference on healing prayer led by Francis and Judith MacNutt.

It was a great two-day conference, and toward the end the speakers said, "We know some of you have hurts and needs. If that's you, just come up to the front and we'll pray for you." Many went forward, and you could see by the expressions on their faces and the movements of their bodies that God was working in them.

I decided to go up front for prayer. At this point I knew that I was the problem—actually, I think I always knew—and that I needed help. Francis MacNutt put his hands on me, and I felt absolutely nothing. I went back to my seat and sat down next to Peggy. I saw her looking at me out of the corner of her eyes. I'm sure she was praying, hoping, begging for God to do something. But I felt nothing. *Perfect,* I thought to myself, *just like everything else in my life.*

Amazingly, the next morning when I woke up, all of the bitterness, anger, and darkness was gone. It was just like being born again. I didn't say anything to Peggy because I thought, *Maybe I'm imagining it; maybe it will go away in a couple of weeks; maybe I'll mess this up too.* But it didn't go away. After a couple of months I finally said to Peggy, "I think I'm changed. I think God has healed me." And she said, "I know he has. I knew before we left California."

People get lost from God—all of us are lost before we come to know him; some of us feel lost after we come to know him. Being lost from God causes us to do all kinds of things that make us difficult and ugly and hard to love. So when I remember that part of my story and how much I needed someone to love me—the way that Peggy did—and how much I needed a God who wouldn't give up on me, it makes it easier for me to love others when they need someone who will be with them and not walk away.

When we're honest with ourselves and remember our stories—recalling the pain we felt and the mistakes we made—we're no longer tempted to think, "Why don't they straighten up and do right?" Instead, we say to ourselves, "Thank God for the grace that saved me and for the chance now to give that grace to others."

We all are human. We all have a story. We all get lost and need to be found. We all become wounded and need to be healed. We all are sinful and in need of grace. We all need someone to assure us that God is with us. We all are in this thing called life—with its wonders and its horrors—together. And our faith in Jesus should make us identify with lost and hurting people more, not less.

Remember your story—what it was like to be without God or to feel far from God, struggling with loneliness, confusion, and pain. Remembering your story will help you to be *with* others. If we are going to be the body of Christ, then we must be the presence of God with people in this world.

We Must Care About Others' Stories

When we tell people that God is with them and they can trust their lives to Jesus, we are asking them to trust us. Essentially we are telling them that we can show them how to create a different ending to their story. We are saying and promising, "Trust us with your lives; trust us with your stories. We will take you to the One who loves you. Trust us; we will not disappoint you."

You don't earn that kind of trust by telling people how badly they have lived or by acting superior. You earn that kind of trust by caring enough about their stories that you want their hopes and dreams to be redeemed. You earn that kind of trust by demonstrating humility and compassion as Jesus did—who was willing to leave the comforts of heaven and be born in a manger, disappointed by friends, rejected by the masses, and crucified on a cross—so that you can make the lives of others better.

"Trust us." When we point people to Jesus, that's what we're asking them to do. We're saying, "Trust us. We will take you to the One who loves you. We will not grow weary of you, disappoint you, or leave you. Trust us with your story. We will be in it with you, help you to rewrite it, and with God's help, make it a better story, full of redemption and hope."

What enables people to trust us is our genuine care for their lives and their stories. And most often, what changes people is love. Most people are not argued into the Kingdom, lectured into the Kingdom, or guilted into the Kingdom. Most people are loved into the Kingdom.

Think about it. When someone gives us the gift of love by the way they look at us, how they listen to us, what they say or do for us, or when they refuse to walk away even when we are mean or selfish or out of control—then we begin to feel safe enough to be real, letting them see us for who we really are. And if they love us even then, the most remarkable thing can happen: we can begin to believe that God loves us too—and we can love ourselves. That is when we can quit hiding or lying about who we are and admit—both to ourselves and to God—our guilt, brokenness, and shame, trusting that God is with us and has the grace in his heart to forgive us. It all begins with love and compassion—with someone seeing us for who we are and choosing to be with us.

It took more than a baby
in a manger to save a race of
sinners. It took a Savior on
a cross. No life is saved and
no story is redeemed unless
someone cares enough to
be willing to go to a cross.

This is who we are as the body of Christ—the ones who care about the stories of others, the ones who can be trusted, the ones who love others the way that Jesus loves us.

Of course, caring—real caring—is always costly. That's what we see in Jesus. It took more than a baby in a manger to save a race of sinners. It took a Savior on a cross. No life is saved and no story is redeemed unless someone cares enough to be willing to go to a cross.

Being with people the way Jesus was with people means suffering with them and for them. It means not walking away when we are rebuffed and rejected. It means continuing to care when we are misjudged and mistreated.

Some people will take a long time to reach, but all people matter to God; and so they must matter to us. We must persevere in caring for others even when there is a price to pay.

People want to believe in the wonder of Christmas. They want to believe there is a God who knows them and cares about them. They want to believe there is an Immanuel, a God who is with them. My prayer is that we will live in such a way that they will know the promise is true. Wherever they are, however they struggle—no matter how far they have wandered or how much they hurt—the promise is true: "The virgin will conceive a child! She will give birth to a son and will call him Immanuel (which means 'God is with us')" (Isaiah 7:14 NLT).

One of the wonders of Christmas is that the promise of Immanuel is as real today as it was two millennia ago. The One who came to be with shepherds and sinners on Christmas night continues to come to be with us two thousand years later. Christmas is more than a story of what once happened. It is a wondrous invitation for us to experience the reality and the power of God ourselves. Christmas is the assurance that no matter how far we have strayed, how low we have fallen, how deeply we have been hurt, or how others may see us, God has come not to judge us or condemn us but to be with us. The risen Christ promised that the wonder of Christmas would continue. He said, "Here I am! I stand at the door and knock. If anyone hears my voice and opens the door, I will come in" (Revelation 3:20 NIV).

Christmas is not only the story of what once happened but also the story of what is happening now. Open your heart to the wonder of Christmas so that you can experience its reality and power and claim the promise for yourself!

REFLECT

How does the promise of Christmas—that in Jesus Christ, God is Immanuel—God with you today, tomorrow, and forever—give you hope and peace for your life right now?

_____

_____

_____

_____

_____

_____

_____

_____

What are some practical ways you can "keep" the promise of Christmas this season—making it real in the lives of others by being the presence of God to those who are confused, hurting, or lost?

_____

_____

_____

_____

_____

_____

_____

_____

How can recalling your own story help you to show compassion to others, loving them as Jesus has loved you? Invite God to bring to mind a part of your story that you need to remember this Christmas.

_____

_____

_____

_____

_____

_____

_____

MEDITATE

"The virgin will conceive and give birth to a son, and they will call him Immanuel" (which means "God with us").

Matthew 1:23 NIV

But when the fullness of the time came, God sent forth His Son, born of a woman, born under the Law, so that He might redeem those who were under the Law, that we might receive the adoption as sons. Because you are sons, God has sent forth the Spirit of His Son into our hearts, crying, "Abba! Father!" Therefore you are no longer a slave, but a son; and if a son, then an heir through God.

Galatians 4:4-7 NASB

Seeing the people, He felt compassion for them, because they were distressed and dispirited like sheep without a shepherd.

Matthew 9:36 NASB

"And surely I am with you always, to the very end of the age."

Matthew 28:20b NIV

PRAY

Lord Jesus, today I stand in awe with a heart full of gratitude at the wonder of your promise to be Immanuel—God with us today, tomorrow, and forever. You are a God who truly understands our struggles, because you lived in our world and experienced life in the same ways that we do. You have compassion on us, recognizing that we are sheep in need of a tender shepherd. Help me to have that same compassion for others, reaching out to love them just as you have loved me. With your help, I will seek to "keep" the promise of Christmas—not only this season but all of my days. Amen.

ADVENT WREATH READING
THE FOURTH SUNDAY OF ADVENT

Christmas Story Element: Promise

Theme: Joy

Scripture: Matthew 1:18-23

Light the Wreath:

In anticipation of the coming Christ, light the fourth candle in your Advent wreath; then light the other three candles you've lit previously.

Reflect:

Today we wish for the world to know the promise fulfilled in our king, the prince of peace, the wonderful counselor, and we declare, "Many.../are the wonders you have done,/the things you planned for us.../too many to declare" (Psalm 40:5). As we reflect on the wonder of the promise of Christmas, we thank God that all of his promises to us are fulfilled in the birth, life, and death of Jesus; and we rejoice in God's faithful love, which brings us immeasurable joy.

Today, focus on the joy that is ours in the promised Christ, God with us.

Pray:

God of promise, thank you for sending Jesus to fulfill all of your promises to us. Show us ways that we can keep the promise of Christmas by being your hands and feet in the lives of others. Amen.

Notes

Chapter 1: The Wonder of a Star

1. Frederick Buechner, "The Face in the Sky," *The Hungering Dark* (San Francisco: HarperSanFrancisco, 1969), 13.
2. *The Free Dictionary*, s.v. "Magi," accessed June 3, 2016, http://encyclopedia2.thefreedictionary.com /Magoi.
3. John H. Hopkins Jr., "We Three Kings," *The United Methodist Hymnal* (Nashville: The United Methodist Publishing House, 1989), 254.

Chapter 2: The Wonder of a Name

1. *Strong's Concordance Online*, s.v. "Hoshea," accessed June 7, 2016, http://biblehub.com /hebrew/1954.htm.

2. *Strong's Concordance Online*, s.v. "Yhvh" (Jehovah), accessed June 7, 2016, http://biblehub .com/hebrew/3068.htm.

3. *Strong's Concordance Online*, s.v. "Yehoshua," accessed June 7, 2016, http://biblehub.com /hebrew/3091.htm.

Chapter 3: The Wonder of a Manger

1. *Strong's Concordance Online*, s.v. "Kataluma," accessed June 14, 2016, http://biblehub.com /greek/2646.htm.

2. Tim Chaffey, "Born in a Barn (Stable)?" *Answers in Genesis*, November 30, 2010, accessed June 21, 2016, https://answersingenesis.org/holidays /christmas/born-in-a-barn-stable/.

3 . Benjamin Schäfer, "God's Pursuit of Man," *A Yearning Heart's Journey Blog*, accessed June 21, 2016, http://yearningheartsjourney.blogspot .com/2014/01/gods-pursuit-of-man.html.

4. Charles Wesley, "And Can It Be That I Should Gain," *The United Methodist Hymnal* (Nashville: The United Methodist Publishing House, 1989), 363.

5. E. Stanley Jones, "On Christian Meditation" in *Abundant Living* (Nashville: Abingdon Press, 2014), n.p.

6. William Richard Ezell, "Incarnation: When Jesus Stepped Out", *Preaching.com*, November 1, 1997. Accessed June 22, 2016, http://www.preaching .com/sermons/11563927/.

7. History.com staff, "D-Day," *History.com*, accessed June 22, 2016, http://www.history.com/topics /world-war-ii/d-day.

8. Darrell Johnson, "The Sleepy Invasion," *Preaching Today.com*, accessed June 22, 2016, http://www. preachingtoday.com/sermons/sermons/2005 /august/039.html?start=7.

9. Ibid.

10. David J. Kalas, "God's Sneak Attack," in *Sermons on the Gospel Readings*, J. Ellworth Kalas et. al. (Lima, OH: CSS Publishing Company, Inc., 2003), 42.

11. Story taken from Will Fish, "A Russian Christmas Story: For Always," *Eternal Perspective Ministries with Randy Alcorn*, December 1, 1999, accessed June 23, 2016, http://www.epm.org/ resources/1999/Dec/1/russian-christmas-story -always/.

12. Ibid.

13. Ibid.

14. Benjamin Schäfer, http://yearningheartsjourney. blogspot.com/2014/01/gods-pursuit-of-man.html.